One More Sunset, Maybe I'd Be Satisfied

Front cover artwork, "Corner Sunset in the Quarter," by Evelyn M. Huckaby, © 2007.

Back cover photography by Dennis Huckaby, © 2008.

All stories © 2008 by Evelyn M. Huckaby.

Without limiting the rights under copyright reserved above, no part of this publication may be reproduced, stored in or introduced into a retrieval system, or transmitted, in any form or by any means (electronic, mechanical, photocopying, recording, or otherwise), without the prior written permission of the copyright owners and the publisher of this book.

ISBN: 978-0-615-25841-6

Contents

Acknowledgements. 7

From Bourbon Street to Esplanade.. 9

Our House in the Middle of Our Street 17

I Fall to Pieces 25

Slippin', Into the Future... 29

Going to the Chapel and We're Going to Get Married 31

I Got Bugs in My Room, Bugs in My Pocket, and Bugs in My Shoes 35

Holy, Holy, Holy.. 37

Nobody Knows the Trouble I've Seen 41

I Never Promised You a Rose Garden 45

Jambalaya, Crawfish Pie, File' Gumbo! 49

It's Up to You, New York, New York 53

Nothing More Than Feelings 57

I'm A Red-Necked Woman, Not Some High Class Broad......................... 59

And She'll Have Fun, Fun, Fun Till Her Daddy Takes Her T-Bird Away, ...
Or Was It a Corvette? 63

Time Keeps On Slippin' 67

I Went Sky Diving, I Went Rocky Mountain Climbing 71

Uptown Girl... 75

Love, Sweet Love 77

I Scream, You Scream, We All Scream.. 81

Bit By Bit, Putting It Together.. 83

When the Moon Hits Your Eye Like a Big Pizza Pie.. 87

It's The Most Wonderful Time of the Year... 89

Put Your Behind in Your Past.. 91

I See It in Your Eyes, Maybe It Was Better Left Unsaid...................................... 93

When I Was Young, I'd Listen to the Radio 97

Are You Going To Scarborough Fair?... 101

Birds Do It, Bees Do It, Even Monkeys in the Trees Do It................................ 105

It's a Beautiful Ride.. 109

Painted Candy Canes on the Tree 113

Tiny Tots With Their Eyes All Aglow... 119

I Saw Mommy Kissing Santa Claus And Other Parental Delusions 121

Life Is a Highway... 125

Living Is Easy With Eyes Closed.... Strawberry Fields Forever........................ 127

Kiss My Tiara... 131

Though At Heart I'm a Pearl, I'm a Difficult Girl, So, Buddy, Beware 135

My Son Turned Ten Just the Other Day 137

For a Moment Like This, Some People Wait a Lifetime 139

Acknowledgements

I would like to thank those in my life who said years ago that there were stories inside me that needed to be told and who helped me believe I should be the one to tell them.

I must also give thanks to our family friend Timothy Waldrop, without whom I would not have finished this book.

A very big thank you goes to my dear friend Julia Forbes for providing me with a title for this work.

Many thanks to my friend Judy Terrase for all of her encouragement and for making me laugh out loud every single day.

Lastly, and most importantly, I would like to thank my husband, Dennis Huckaby, for taking all the pieces of my life and making them a beautiful whole. He, and my two sons, Thomas and Benjamin, are my treasures in this life. My wish is to have just one more sunset with them.

For Phyllis, my friend always.

1

From Bourbon Street to Esplanade

"Help us!" was scrawled in large white letters on the rooftop of a squat apartment building alongside the interstate a year ago as I drove through New Orleans. Block after block, ramshackled and weather-worn shotgun houses leaned this way and that on their foundations. Sprayed like graffiti, circles and cross marks could still be seen on the front of each house. They are reminders of would-be rescuers who came through our deserted city in the days and weeks after Hurricane Katrina. Yet, when I recall my birthplace, no Hurricane Katrinas mar the memory. No dilapidated houses litter the scenes in my mind, and no deserted streets fill my thoughts. The New Orleans of my childhood was a magical place of happy music, exotic smells, delicious food, and good friends and neighbors.

As children, we had such freedom to play and to live. We could leave the house in the morning and not return until the streetlights came on at dusk. That's when dad would get home and momma would have supper cooked. My Aunt Phyllis and I would ride our bicycles everywhere. She's only a few years older than I, and she got an allowance when we were young. She was rich in my mind. I didn't get an allowance, but my grandfather took pity on me and would give me a quarter when I'd visit.

The very first place we'd go was to the corner store for a coke ICEE. There were little diamonds on the sides of the cup, and if you saved enough of them, you could get your ICEE for around 10 or 15 cents. From there, we'd hold on to our frozen coke treat and ride our bikes out of the subdivision and over to the GTX store.

No one minded that two children were coming to the store alone. We'd leave our bicycles out on the sidewalk and spend the next hour or so wandering around the toy section. There was one unattainable toy I always wanted. I'd find it each time we'd go to the store and I would hold it and read all the packaging and fine print. I wanted the Sea Monkeys. Who knew what a fantastical thing something as simple as brine shrimp could be? With those Sea Monkeys, I could enter a tiny magical world, I could have little friends, and I could watch life growing and dancing before me. I never got the Sea Monkeys, but I did get the Magic Rocks. Someone gave them to me for my birthday. I kept them in a glass mayonnaise jar and they lasted for years.

Momma used to shop at the old Canal Villere on Veteran's Blvd. Phyllis and I loved it when she'd go there since they had the best buggies in all of the city. The buggies were tall with a big crawl space under them where a child could sit, were a child so inclined. I was that child. Phyllis and I would get a buggy together, and momma would go shopping. The only time momma ever knew what we were doing in the store was when the store manager walked us over to her and proceeded to tell her that Phyllis was pushing me very fast in the buggy before letting go, after which I would go sailing through the cross aisles, hitting people or displays. It was so much fun. Mom kept us close for the rest of the shopping trip, but the next time, we were back to racing through the aisles. She was far braver than I, and my shrieks and screams only made her run faster.

At that same Canal Villere, I got one of the worst spankings I can remember. My momma is terribly afraid of spiders. As she was checking out all her groceries, Phyllis and I wandered over to the little vending machines, where, for a penny or nickel, you could get a tattoo, a big purple gum ball, or a keychain. On this particularly fateful day, Phyllis found a soft, floppy, hairy, plastic spider. A big one. It was on the floor under the little gumball machine. She pocketed the spider and hatched a plan to scare my mom. Momma was eating potato chips out of a large can she'd just purchased, and the plan was for me to ask her if I could have a potato chip. Upon getting the can from mom, I handed it to Phyllis and she reached in like she was getting a chip, only she deposited the spider inside and replaced the lid. I was to hand the can back to momma and high-tail it back over to the gumball machine.

I'd barely gotten back to the rendezvous point when the trouble started. My mother screamed long and loud and threw that can of potato chips straight up in the air. When the spider landed, the cashier started screaming and then all the women around started screaming. Phyllis and I were almost bent over laughing. Finally someone realized it was a joke, and with tears on her face and murder in her eyes, momma finished checking out.

I knew I was in for it big time. We reached the car and she grabbed a piece of plastic piping off her vinyl car seat and started pulling. When she'd ripped off about 3 feet, she commenced to using it to tear my butt up. I was crying and yelling and telling her that it was Phyllis' idea, but since Phyllis was her little sister and not her child, she couldn't lay a hand on her. I got a double portion of butt-whoopin'. Phyllis still laughs about it to this day.

In my elementary years, New Orleans had begun to desegregate the schools. All my friends' parents were in a tizzy about whether to switch to private schools rather than allowing their kids to attend school with black children. I recall my mother teaching me to be friendly *toward* black people, but not to be friends *with* black people. It simply wasn't done. Following the same route as many other families, my parents enrolled us in Kehoe Academy, a prestigious (translated "white") private school in the city. Apparently my parents felt that either private school was too expensive or black people weren't very dangerous, because we only attended Kehoe for one semester. Back we went to public school.

I went to Westgate Elementary, and I remember distinctly how exciting it was at school to get the first King Cake each year after Christmas. Whoever found the small plastic baby in the cake had to buy the next one. I never got the baby, but that's probably a good thing, because I doubt my parents would have bought a cake for my class. I do remember those cakes our class would get would be huge; they were big enough for everybody in the class to have some for two days. They weren't filled with anything like they are today, and I don't recall the glaze being white like some places make it now. The glaze was clear, with the gold, purple, and green sugars providing the only color on the top. It's so good, surely it must be a sin.

There are only a few years we went to Mardi Gras in the Quarter. When I was young, it seemed family-oriented, despite the nearly-naked people, and the old man who peed freely in the street. My dad's parents were always the King and Queen of whichever Krewe was popular at the time. There were pictures in my grandfather's office of them dressed up in the most elaborate costumes, faces covered in masks, feathers sticking out of the tops of their heads, and sequins covering their clothes. As I'd sit in my grandfather's office, I'd pretend to be their long-lost princess daughter. Some dreams don't come true, I've found.

Somewhere there is a painting of me as a three year old. My mom and dad and I had gone to Jackson Square on a Saturday morning as we frequently did. A man with a camera was walking around the square and told my mom and dad that if they would let him photograph me, he'd send them all the copies. The painting looked awful, but the pictures the man eventually sent were adorable. I looked like a little Shirley Temple, with curly light brownish-blonde hair and pouty little lips. Back then, the photographer was just a man enthralled with the beauty of a small child. Nowadays, we'd probably think he was a pervert.

Saturdays at Jackson Square always began at Cafe du Monde. I would get covered head to toe with the powdered sugar from those beignets we'd get with our white mugs of cafe au lait. To this day, I cannot drink coffee like grown people; it must be half cream or milk and half coffee, and very sweet. It's a taste I love from childhood.

People from all over the world would walk past that outdoor café. Old black men would stand on the sidewalk and play tubas and trumpets for the spare change people would toss into strategically-placed empty wine boxes. Sometimes an enthusiastic couple would dance right there in the street as the musicians played. The air was filled with the sounds of happy laughter, countless jazz melodies, and tugboats on the nearby river. The sun would be up and hot in the morning and families would ride past in horse-drawn buggies. I was always excited to see the way the horses were decorated with straw hats and wreaths of flowers. They were as colorful as any painted lady on Bourbon Street.

Afterward, we'd walk along the levy at a place where we could see the riverboats floating by with their load of tourists. I can close my eyes and hear the calliopes playing loudly even now. When I was in 5th grade, one of our field trips included a ride on a riverboat. I will never forget kissing Paul Duvet on the middle deck near the mist from the paddlewheel. It was magical with little rainbows everywhere from the sunshine pouring through the mist as the paddlewheel slapped the river again and again.

Life has found me living in Baton Rouge now, but there is a part of me that desires to spend long afternoons walking through the Quarter, browsing through quaint bookstores and antique shops, or even braving the voodoo shops and Musee Conti Wax Museum. I want to go back to City Park and I want to ride my bicycle by the lake. I want to sashay by.

Across the street from the French Market

2

Our House in the Middle of Our Street

I've had a great deal of time over the last couple of years to contemplate my evolving ties with my mother. Those very real ties have been evident more now than at any other time in my life, due to my parents moving next door to me. Out of the blue, after living in another state for years, they decided to buy the house directly next to mine. This event prompted me feigning several attempts at suicide with a very dull butter knife. I watched from my kitchen window as truck after truck arrived with box after box, quickly filling up the rooms of their new home. As I watched, I began to remember all the places I'd lived with my parents through the years.

My mother was raised by the gypsies and I'm from everywhere. At least that is what I say when asked where I'm from. For reasons I've yet to fully understand, after living all over New Orleans, my parents moved us from state to state, country to city, over and over again, during all the years I lived at home. I don't recall a time I ever went to the same school two years in a row except for 8th and 9th grade. Even though most of our moves were in and around New Orleans, every year there were new faces and a new city, as my parents were always searching, I suppose, for a place they could somehow be happy together.

Momma said when I was young that dad was like hurricane season, except when the hurricanes came, dad left. Maybe that explains a lot of the moving we did. Though I remember him being gone many times in my childhood, I only clearly remember a few of the times he said goodbye. The year I was 10, he and momma separated again and I remember vividly momma giving me her wedding rings to bring outside to my father. I didn't understand why he was going. I didn't understand why I felt so very alone. I always wondered if dad were leaving because of something I'd done, and even now, my life is spent trying very hard not to disappoint people for fear they'll walk away from me. Days before he left, mother had another emotionally-charged meltdown and threw all of our dishes onto the tile floor in the kitchen. I stood watching with the terrified confusion of a child.

During this particularly huge fight, I also watched her throw every one of her African Violets onto the floor - dirt and glass and water and plants flying everywhere. It broke my heart. Momma had worked so hard on the ceramic planters for those delicate flowers. The containers were all so beautiful; they were some of the prettiest things in our little house. But they were destroyed amidst the screaming and arguing and insanity that were a part of life during those years.

We eventually moved to be near my grandparents on the edge of a river in the swamps of Louisiana. The most thrilling part of living in the swamp was the yearly flood. The river would rise and the water around us would come up around our trailer so high, we could sit in the window and hang our feet down and touch the water. We'd get down on the floor and look through the floor vents at the spiders and minnows going by in the water. Water moccasins would float by, schools of fish looked as big and dark as whales, but the fun was over when dad would row us in the pirogue to the bridge and then drive us to school - I always felt it was patently unfair to make us give up a day of swimming in the flood water.

There's nothing like sitting in your bedroom window watching the neighbor's patio table and chairs and garbage and wading pool float past you. It was fascinating to see whole mounds of ants floating in the water. The bottom ants sacrifice themselves for the rest of the colony and the fire ants would live on. I was always terrified that the mound would bump up against our little trailer and in pure Sunday-afternoon-science-fiction-movie-fashion, we'd be surrounded and eaten by mutant ants. Fortunately, we were spared all but the fears of over-active imaginations.

For all that Momma wanted to live next to her own momma, they didn't get along very well. It wasn't unusual for one or the other to leave torn up pictures of each other on the doorstep after a big fight. They were always screaming at each other, "You are DEAD to me, DEAD, do you hear me?!" Most of this was spawned by the attention and love PaPaw gave to my Momma, and my grandmother was jealous. After having two boys, she'd had my mother, and until my Aunt Phyllis came along very late in my grandparent's lives, Momma was the apple of her daddy's eye. PaPaw never had much time for his wife, but he loved his daughters. The fact that my grandmother was an insane woman could have had something to do with this. MaMaw was 'committed' on several occasions - I don't know how many - and twice, she had electric shock treatments. MaMaw's electric shock treatments were the topic of many scintillating conversations around our dinner table, as one can imagine.

For many of my growing up years, my great-grandmother, known to me as Big Mamaw, lived nearby. Well, not exactly nearby, but close enough for Phyllis and me to ride our bicycles over there. Her house was made of wood throughout, and we could entertain ourselves for hours going from room to room through the connecting closet passageways. We just knew those closets were secret spying passages for Big Mamaw to watch us. How else could she know all the trouble we were into? In the front yard was a three foot statue of the Virgin Mary, and inside the house, there was a little shrine built for her. There were burning candles, little rosaries, statues of Jesus and Mary and frankly, I still find the whole thing a little scary.

Because Big Mamaw was so concerned for our mortal souls and devilish ways, she'd bring Phyllis and me to church with her. Phyllis, all of four years older than me, led me further into temptation, and I'm sorry to say, I was the recipient of many painful pinchings on the leg from Big Mamaw. Phyllis could find something funny in anything, and the day we laughed out loud over the funny faces made by the knots in the wood of the pew in front of us, was the last time my great-grandmother brought us with her. Apparently we either didn't need saving all that much, or else she decided she wasn't the one to do it. The priest was none too happy with us, either.

~~~~~~~~~

I've often missed those long and lazy days in the country when there was nothing in the whole world better to do than to walk barefoot down the gravel road and look for wildflowers. I don't know that I could ever recreate such a feeling of 'no cares in the world' again. It is an innocence I dearly pine for as an adult. MaMaw had a porch swing, and I could lie there to my heart's content. When Phyllis got through with her chores, (she was older than me and naturally had more chores, except when she could talk me into doing them for her) we would make mayonnaise sandwiches and walk across the street to the Gonzales' property. The

Gonzales family only came to their camp on the weekends during the summer, so, during the week, it was ours to run. We'd walk to the end of their pier, sit down, and let our feet hang in the water. I was always afraid of water moccasins, but I let my feet hang anyway, because it was so cooling to have them in the moving water. We'd sit there and wave at the neighbors as they passed by on boats. We'd wave at everyone - there were no strangers, and everyone would wave back, just like they knew who we were. When boats would go by fast, we loved it because the water would lap up on our legs.

Oddly enough, when we moved back to the city, so did my grandparents. Or maybe I have it backwards and my parents followed instead. Regardless, this meant my one best friend was with me again: Phyllis. I don't really remember any other best friends when I was very young. Phyllis and I were the terror of the neighborhood, or I should say, Phyllis was the terror and I was her mostly non-willing accomplice. She quickly discovered that I would follow suit into any trouble she could find. She found a lot. I'll never forget the afternoon she rolled up her sleeves and told me, "Ev, go get MaMaw. I'm about to beat the crap out of Normee Simoneaux." I ran like all the civilized world depended on me running fast. MaMaw and I got back just in time to watch Phyllis lay Normee out flat. Phyllis could beat up most anybody, including the boys. Nobody ever made the mistake of crossing her twice.

I think there was a certain rebel streak in Phyllis she'd be quite proud of if I ever mentioned it to her. She pushed the edge. I think she embodied for me, a scared and timid child, all that was brave. Around her, I was somebody. And she protected me. When my Uncle Waverly 'fooled around with me,' Phyllis made me tell Momma. Of course, it did no good because back then, nobody ever talked about the fact that a child's innocence was wiped away in an afternoon. She just put her arm around me and vowed to kill Waverly if he ever touched me again. I believed her. It was unfortunate for me that she wasn't around later to spare me the curiosity of my father.

3

I Fall to Pieces

For most of my adult life, I have been unable to comprehend exactly what it is that simmered beneath the surface of my heart when dealing with my parents. There was so much deep-seated anger and resentment stemming from my childhood. A few years ago, at the time my parents moved next door to us, I started to understand. We began experiencing problems with my youngest son. He seemed to show signs of possible abuse, and as any parent would do, I tried to gently pry information from him. One night, after praying with him before bedtime, I asked once more what was on his heart and mind. His quiet and timid words chilled me: "Papaw has evil hands." I almost threw up.

My youngest has always been extra-sensitive. He's our animal lover, our tree hugger, our vegetarian. If what I suspected were true, I knew he would be traumatized. In those few seconds of shock, as he uttered the words that would change my world, total clarity reigned in my mind. Somehow I had buried the memories of the molestation by my father when I was 13; I'd somehow filed it away in the filing cabinet drawer of my mind right beside the sexual abuse by my uncle. I suppose there are some things in this life that are too ugly to look at head-on, and the mind has to find a way to cope with what it does not wish to accept. Now I was being forced to open that closed drawer and reexamine its contents. I was repulsed and terrified by what I saw through these adult eyes.

When I was in sixth grade, we moved away from the city for good. Life was happy out in the country. Things were peaceful. Things were quiet. On our gravel road, only the occasional car driving by would disturb the sound of the wind in the trees and insects buzzing by. My sister and I played with Barbie dolls outside, while my brother would play with the large pile of bricks we had stacked by a tree. We'd ride our bikes on the gravel road and we'd play along the edges of the river, trying to catch minnows and tadpoles. Life was slower and simpler and our days were dotted with "don't let the screen door slam!" and "you kids go play outside!" I can see now that innocence is sometimes only a façade, while gentle ways and manners sometimes only serve as a flimsy mask.

Monthly, my father would drive me into New Orleans for my orthodontist's appointment. I was born with far too many teeth for my mouth and it was determined that only the most heinous-looking braces and head gear would solve my problems. It was during one of these trips home across Lake Ponchartrain that he molested me. I felt filthy dirty. Boys weren't supposed to touch your body. Fathers weren't supposed to touch your body. I moved away from him in the front seat of the car and wouldn't look at his face. The person who was supposed to engender trust in my heart had just become a sexual being to me. I went to my mother when we got home and told her what had occurred. I thought she would be so angry with me for letting something like that happen, but she wasn't. I can only assume she threatened him in some way, because we never spoke of it again. Not ever. I was 13.

"Papaw has evil hands." I can still hear his little-boy voice speaking those words with trembling lips. I almost couldn't breathe. My every waking thought during those days was of what could be happening with my son. He began therapy and the only thing we could determine is that, after my parents moved next door, my father would frequently hold my son very tightly and would tickle him. My father was a near-stranger to my son, and the aggressiveness was terrifying. My son would cry when my father would pick him up to do this. It was only later when I began researching 'tickling' that I came across articles which showed child abusers will often use it as a way of gaining physical and emotional control over a young child. It certainly doesn't happen in every case, but there was an undeniable link between the two - a link I could not ignore.

During this time, I confronted my father. "I remember what you did to me." Those were some of the hardest words I had ever said to him. He cried, he stammered, he apologized, and then he did the unthinkable: he tried to justify and explain it. "You have to understand, I was just curious about your developing body. You were growing up and changing and I wanted to see what was happening." I am sickened and repulsed to this day over his comments.

My mother's words at the time were as deeply wounding. "How could you try and destroy our lives now? I'm sorry, very, very sorry, this happened to you. I hoped all my life you would forget it happened. But, why now? Why after all these years? Don't you know your father would lose his job over this? And for God's sake, how could you think your father would do something to your son?" I thought to myself, well, maybe it was because the situation had precedence. She would intermittently forget that if he had abused me, it was altogether possible he could have done it to my son, too. It was only after I assured her I was not pressing charges against my father for his actions toward me that she began to stop questioning me. I felt that as soon as she knew their lifestyle wasn't being threatened, she backed down.

I learned a lot about mothering that day. I learned a lot about myself.

4

Slippin', Into the Future

Time passes, as it is wont to do, and often old wounds are healed, or at the very least, scabbed over where you can pick at them again and again. That seems to best describe the ensuing days as our two families attempted to pull together and overcome our differences over the past several years. Life began to alternate between quick trips through our backyards as either momma or I would venture over to see the other's flower gardens, and times of staring silently at each others' home out our kitchen windows wondering why we were so angry with one another all the time.

Throughout my adult life, I've tried very hard to deal with situations which came up between momma and me as one would deal with a very young child. I understood the serious difficulties my mother faced growing up, and knew those difficulties were the very reasons she behaved as she did as an adult. In an unanswered letter, I'd once asked my father to please find some way to help her. She deserves to live a happy and fulfilled life, as well as a life full of people she loves. Instead, because of her fears and general insecurities, I've always felt that momma lives her life lashing out at the very people who love her in an attempt not to be hurt by them first. Her life is instead filled with belongings, not people, because people will hurt you or disappoint you. I suppose that sometimes, there's just only so much you can handle in your life.

Living in such close proximity means I am often the target of my mother's unhappiness. Then again, she is often unfairly the target of mine. I don't know what will bring true reconciliation and acceptance between us. I don't know that anything can or will make everything all better.

I want to believe there will be more days of sitting on her back porch with coffee in hand listening to stories of her growing up poor in the South. I want to believe there will be more times I'll hear of the antics of her old neighbors Guisse and Oustant. I want to know there will be another day I'll say the words, "Tell me again, momma…. about anything."

5

Going to the Chapel and We're Going to Get Married

Dennis, my husband, has been a photographer for as long as I've known him. His grandfather owned a small studio in Baton Rouge in the 1960s, and as a young man, my husband would go with Papa to take pictures at various weddings in and around town. When I married into the family, it was only natural that I would tag along, too.

I loved to watch Papa use his old Hasselblad camera. This camera is held at chest level and to look down into it only shows you your subject matter upside down. I still get woozy just thinking about trying to focus in such an unusual way, but Papa could work that camera quick as lightning. As he got older he began to lose his balance, though, which is evidenced by the fact that in my own wedding photos, nearly everyone is leaning to the left in all the shots.

Eventually, the business fell to my husband and I became his able and willing assistant. Soon enough, as I would set up a picture for him and then eventually see the results of the picture in the developed film, I began to get frustrated when his photos didn't turn out the way I'd seen them in my mind. One day, in exasperation (I can cause that at times, I'm sorry to say) he handed me the camera and said if I thought I could do better, do it. When my developed pictures came back, he shut right up. They were beautiful. They were exactly what I'd seen in my mind when setting the shot. We soon learned to work as a team with him handling all the technical aspects of the picture taking, and me handling all the creativity.

We don't really have a 'business' per se, and while word-of-mouth gets us as much work as we can handle, it also gets us to some rather interesting places. Take the case of the Nascar wedding.

We drove way out in the country on a late Friday afternoon, with the day already dark because of the lateness of the season. As we pulled up to the church, tiki torches were burning bright enough for us to spot a group of long-side-burned, mullet-haired guys in jeans and Nascar jackets decorating a pickup truck with condoms and toilet paper. We later learned that the pickup belonged to the bride. I looked over at my husband and the unspoken words between us screamed, "Rednecks." I am not certain why the inner "tacky" of some people surfaces when it comes time for a wedding.

Since we always take pictures of the reception hall ahead of time, we were able to see first hand what Nascar decorations look like. There were flags standing and hanging everywhere, the tables were covered in black and white checkered patterns, little matchbox cars were on the tables, and the bridesmaids were running around in, well, Nascar apparel. This could all have been tastefully done (I'm not sure how), but, I'm sorry to say, it wasn't.

We wandered around taking pictures of the black and white wedding cake and decorations when, all of a sudden, SWEETFANCYMOSESWHATISTHAT???!!! I slinked around the groom's cake, not getting too close, studying it from this angle and that, trying to decide if it was really…. could it be… tell me it wasn't….. a road-kill armadillo. Oh, yes, it was. Someone had baked a cake and shaped it to be a splayed-out armadillo as if it had been run over in the road. You know, the kind where, as you're driving down the road and you see road kill up ahead and you tell yourself, "I'm not gonna look, I'm not gonna look, I'm not gonna look," but as you get closer and closer, something inside overcomes you and you stare full-on at the horror smashed all on the side of the road because you just can't help yourself? That was the groom's cake. It had little ears made out of Wrigley's chewing gum, and a little pink tongue hanging out, too.

Needless to say, my husband felt this was the neatest thing he'd ever seen in his life. When the cake was served, he nearly knocked people over to be first in line to try a piece. The cake was red velvet and the filling was ooey-gooey red raspberry. I had to choke back the gag reflex and that's saying something for a woman who ate fried alligator in Maurepas last weekend. It tastes like chicken, if you're wondering.

6

I Got Bugs in My Room, Bugs in My Pocket, and Bugs in My Shoes

I have a horrible fear of most insects, with roaches and spiders topping that list. In Louisiana, roaches do not scurry away quickly when bright lights are turned on. No, instead, those 2 ½-inch monsters turn and fly at your head. They instinctively know where the human face is and they go for it.

When I was a young girl, I had to use the bathroom in the middle of the night once, so in the semi-dark I walked the long hallway. I have horrible eyesight and on this night, I wasn't wearing eyeglasses. Something small and dark was on the ceiling and I was a bit wary, but kept going. The roach that had been waiting on our ceiling for some unsuspecting passerby, dove at my head and went straight into my hair. My parents awoke to the screams.

Years later, all grown up and in my own house, I was drawing water for my bath. I needed to use the restroom, so I sat down. A mere five seconds later, a huge roach came running out from the closet straight for my feet. I immediately began screaming and flailing and trying to get away, however, as my feet were tangled in my undies, running away was not possible. I managed several mid-air twists and turns and landed flat on my back in a tub full of water while fully dressed. I hope I gave that roach a heart attack. I sure showed him.

Which brings me to today. I work for a very prestigious company, full of "academic and professional" people. Moments ago, fate visited me a third time – in another restroom, no less. Pantyhose at my ankles, I glanced down to see a large, LARGE black spider crawl onto my shoe and my toe. I can only imagine the horror the very "academic and professional" women at the sinks experienced upon hearing screaming and thrashing and yelling and kicking while watching all the stalls shaking. Then there was silence. It took a moment to compose myself and straighten my flying strands of hair and crumpled clothing. I squared my shoulders, gathered what precious little dignity I had left and walked out. The women were still staring, mouths agape, whispering quietly amongst themselves. Let them talk.

7

Holy, Holy, Holy

Yesterday was a rainy, dreary day – a perfect day for me to make gumbo. I made a lot of it since, not only was I feeding the small army residing at my house during the holidays, I was going to be feeding my mother and father-in-law, as well.

After stopping at the grocery on my way home from work, I walked inside and OHMYGOSH! my house was a disaster. It looked like a centipede lived there because of all the pairs of shoes lying around. No beds were made (except mine upstairs – and let me tell you, my husband was doing all he could to try and keep me happy), food was all over the cabinets, suitcases and clothes were everywhere, etc. Everyone was still off at the bowling alley, spending a day of fun, so I had about an hour to get everything all clean and straightened again.

This could be my house.

After supper, which was outstanding if I do say so myself, I wanted so badly to run upstairs and sneak in a few minutes of "Ugly Betty" and later "Grey's Anatomy." I got neither. Instead, we gathered around for a makeshift magic show and religious discussion. My brother-in-law fancies himself a magician, and I must admit, he was pretty good.

Somewhere during the magic show, we got to talking about the Magic Kingdom and how much I love Disneyland. When I taught school near Los Angeles, I spent my summer at Disneyland and have always longed to go back. "Oh, Evelyn, you need to go to the 'Holy Land Experience' in Orlando instead." That's right, you heard it here first: The Holy Land Experience.

Please don't get me wrong. I have nothing whatsoever against people who go and visit Israel as the birthplace of their faith. I do have something against the commercialization of someone's faith. I guess the whole thing is just really cheesy to me. I mean, do they watch the crucifixion for fun? Hey kids! Let's go watch Jesus die! Bring the popcorn! Oooohhhh! They're showing the Virgin Birth this afternoon at 4!!! (Some material may not be suitable for small children!) At 7, Jesus turns the water into wine!! (Not suitable for anyone under 21!) "Bring Us Barabbas" Burgers will be served until closing. After that, the beheading of John will be held in the courtyard.

I'm truly not trying to be sacrilegious, as, trust me, there is no one more religious than a Southern Baptist gal; there just seems to be something terribly wrong with turning the death of Christ into an amusement park ride. I'm just sayin'.

8

Nobody Knows the Trouble I've Seen

In the Feliciana parishes, along the Mississippi River, some of the most extravagant wealth was accumulated before the Civil War. Three good cotton crops made one a millionaire in those days. After that, the sky was the limit. No opulence was spared, no birdcage left ungilded. One can scarcely comprehend the vastness of these estates, or the beauty and grandeur. "Gone With the Wind" is but a peek into that lifestyle.

Recently my co-workers and I visited Rosedown, a classic plantation dramatically placed at the end of an oak-tree-lined driveway. Those live oaks are over 100 years old, many with their branches sweeping the grounds. We visited Oakley Plantation where John J. Audubon drew his famous birds and wildlife. Next was Grace Episcopal Church where the

Turnbulls donated the enormous and ornate center chandelier in order to establish their wealth among the other church members. We later went on to The Myrtles, one of the most haunted houses in the world.

Lunch was lightly-dusted oven fried catfish, atop a bed of basmati rice, and covered with a spicy crawfish etouffee. Brandy-laced bread pudding topped with mint julep whipped cream finished the meal. There was a live orchestra on the grounds, and we received dancing lessons. My instructor was a very handsome man in tails and a top hat. He wore gloves - be still my southern heart! (I did my best to flutter my eyelashes at all the appropriate times, but that's another story.)

Earlier, while others were viewing the inside of the Oakley Plantation, I wandered around the grounds to the back of the house. I am one of the photographers for our department at the newspaper, so I had the excuse of looking for some good shots. Down a narrow wooded lane, I came to a clearing. I don't know what I was expecting to see, but what I encountered sent shivers down my spine and I stopped cold. I was looking at a row of slave houses. Actually, to call them 'houses' elevates what I saw to something inhabitable, and what I saw wasn't fit for man. Beast maybe, but not man. Growing up in the south makes it impossible for one to ignore race issues. However, what I saw that day went beyond issues of race. What I saw was an issue of inhumanity.

The opulence I'd viewed all day was built on the backs of those people who'd lived in the slave houses. By the age they could carry a bucket, young black children began their lives of slavery. Their homes were smaller than my entire bathroom. All I could think of as I walked cabin to cabin was, "What kind of human enslaves another?" While I walked around on the porches, four black women and a man walked up. All of a sudden, I felt so awkward. I wanted to say to them, "I am so sorry."

I am tired of hearing from others that black people today were never slaves and need to get over it. With my own tormenting issues of my heritage (I've discovered that most of the men on my father's side of the family were KKK) and the way it affects my thinking everyday, I can't imagine what it was like for those five people to stand there and know their ancestors occupied houses like that, lived like that, and died like that. Each of those five are from the area and are descended from slaves. They walked quietly, reverently, as they peeked in windows, stepped up on porches, and ran their hands along worn porch railings. One of the ladies snapped pictures. It was my privilege to gently take the camera from her and photograph them next to the cabins. Afterward, she hugged me and smiled. With never a word spoken, we walked together back to the main house.

Slave quarters at Oakley Plantation

9

I Never Promised You a Rose Garden

My world, my life, and my yard are filled with flowers. I love them, and from the time I got my own home 18 years ago, I have been growing them. I don't always have a lot of success, and most of my plants have to have a will to live in order to survive. Occasionally, upon receiving pot plants as gifts, I've thought to myself, "Well, my little pretty, you aren't long for this world, are you?" I'm usually right, unfortunately.

My mother lives next door to me, and she was born with 10 green fingers and 10 green toes. Everything she touches grows and blooms and does beautiful things. My things will frequently wither and die next to her magnificent specimens. Still, week after week, I get out in my yard, casting tender glances and fertilizer at my plants and flowers, watering and pruning and weeding. Mother's yard has the "Yard of the Month" sign in it. I try not to look at it as I drive by. One day she's going to wake up and that sign is going to be shredded. You didn't hear me say that.

And then there are my daisies. When I got them from the nursery, I tucked them into their soil home with tender loving care. I placed a little, colorful ceramic butterfly next to them. There was such promise that came along with those fat, white heads. Then they didn't grow. I checked for bugs. I watered. I fertilized. I moved them further into the sun. Nothing. Those fat, white heads turned into skinny, scrawny little stalks with flowers a ½ inch wide. My friend, Julia, bought the same daisies. Hers are enormous and could wear bumper stickers that say, "My daisies can beat up your daisies." I can't give up, though. This summer will see me trying yet one more place out for the daisies.

Try as I might, the more I push, the worse those daisies do. On the other hand, I have roses. Lots of them. And every time I walk outside, those bushes are fatter and fuller and have even more roses on them. I neglect them while tending the daisies, and yet the roses prosper. I can't even tell you the last time the roses got fertilizer. But they bloom and bloom despite my seeming neglect. My orange roses are so bright and full, complete strangers stop to see them. And the roses do this on their own.

My oldest son will be leaving home soon. I have been conscious of the fact that he will leave since he's been a child. I've tended him, nurtured him, been "The Meanest Mom In the WHOLE WORLD" sometimes, and fertilized and watered his life. Without me seeing it happen, he's grown into a smart, respectful, hard-working, helpful, responsible, happy young man. He blooms more everyday. He has made a few teenage mistakes, but he has handled them humbly, gracefully, and with wisdom. He is a joy to me. Now I feel as though it's time for me to step back and let him spread his roots a little wider, watching and enjoying the way he grows and thrives. This isn't easy for me. I want to tend him, and letting him loose to grow is difficult. I look forward to the places he will go and the things he will do. Somehow I think he'll be just fine.

10

Jambalaya, Crawfish Pie, Filé Gumbo!

If you live in Louisiana or even visited, you instinctively know that on any given day, at any given time, somebody somewhere is going to be cooking up something good to eat. Probably more than any place in America, Louisiana has fabulous food and good music. It seems like every little town had its own Cajun band. Their music became the backdrop of my life.

If you were fortunate enough to grow up here, you know that food is an intrinsic part of your life's experiences. We had Strawberry Festivals in Ponchatoula in the spring, Jambalaya in Gonzales, Gumbo everywhere in the fall, and Crawfish in very early summer. Actually, there is nearly a festival a week all year long in Louisiana celebrating one food or another.

I have such fond memories of crawfish boils. The men always did the cooking on those days. There would be great pots of boiling, seasoned water, and 50 pound sacks of crawfish would be cooked in a matter of minutes. It was always fun when a stray crawfish wandered away from the pack and gave us something to play with while the grown-ups cooked. When they'd pour out the crawfish pots, everybody would rush to the tables and dig in. Steam would rise from those tables, filling the senses with spices. It always seemed like this was done on sultry, steamy afternoons, and I always ended up with hot juices all over my hands, my arms, and in large drips down my face and neck.

In the fall, momma would start making gumbos. On that first cool morning, we knew gumbo would soon be served at our house. I've already made my first pots of the year, not letting one single early fall morning slip by unnoticed. My favorite is seafood gumbo, and I can remember how momma would fill a big gumbo pot with blue crabs, fat shrimp from the gulf, and oysters. Never in my life have I had anything so good. Usually, though, she'd make chicken and sausage gumbo, using andouille for the sausage. I love filé sprinkled on mine; the more, the better.

I have received several requests for my gumbo recipe. For those of you who don't cook, you can just skip right over this part. For those of you who do, I can promise you a supper you will never forget.

Chicken and Sausage Gumbo

This whole thing needs to cook for a few hours, so don't start it at 5 in the evening if you plan on having it for dinner that night.

Start with a roux (roo). Slowly cook ½ cup flour with ¼ cup (plus a few tablespoons) of vegetable oil. Stir constantly so it does not scorch. It will take about 20-25 minutes for it to reach a deep chocolate color. When it is fairly dark, take it off the burner and set it aside.

Start a big pot of boiling water (it needs to hold about a gallon or more) and add as much chicken as you want to feed your family. For the four of us, I use 8 boneless, skinless thighs. You want enough to have it again the next night. Boil the chicken until it's really cooked. Skim the nasty stuff off the surface of the water. Add 4 or 5 chicken bouillon cubes and a cup and a half of chopped okra and keep boiling it with the chicken.

Sauté the following ingredients gently in a saucepan: Two chopped onions, 1 green bell pepper, 3 or 4 stalks of celery, a few tablespoons of minced garlic, and a few tablespoons of parsley. When the onions are fairly clear, add the whole mixture to the pot of boiling water. I add a few dashes of hot sauce to this and a lot of salt.

When this mixture has boiled for about 30 minutes, I start adding in the roux I cooked. Do NOT ADD IT ALL AT ONE TIME!!!! You will have a big lump if you do. I usually take some of the boiling liquid and add it to the roux first. Then I add a little more. When the roux has 'grown' to where I can't add any more liquid, I start putting the roux back into the pot of boiling water by spoonfuls. Make sure each spoonful is whisked in really well or you'll get lumps.

Next, I add a whole package of either smoked sausage cut up, or a package of andouille, a spicier sausage. Let this mixture simmer all afternoon, at least a couple of hours. The gravy will thicken and become more flavorful because of the roux you've added. You may need some more salt. Keep tasting it.

Make yourself a pot of rice, and after the gumbo has cooked at least 2 hours, put some rice in a bowl and spoon the gumbo over it. I highly recommend sprinkling filè over this in the bowl. DO NOT ADD FILÉ TO THE POT OF GUMBO. It will grow and be disgusting. Only sprinkle it on your own bowl. Serve with French bread and potato salad.

Make this, and your family will love you forever and ever.

11

It's Up to You, New York, New York

I have a rather impulsive personality. That trait has gotten me into trouble on more than one occasion; however, it has also gotten me into some pretty interesting situations, some of which I wouldn't trade for the world.

Several years back, I woke up one morning and decided I wanted to go to New York City. I called my girlfriend, Julia, and asked her if she wanted to go that weekend. After dropping the phone a couple of times and regaining her composure, she said yes, but I had to give her at least a week. Sigh. Some people just have to make plans apparently. So, I spent that week on the computer signing up for free nights at hotels. Neither Julia nor I had any extra money to speak of, and we ended up doing the entire trip from Baton Rouge to New York City and back on $100 each.

I am not a map sort of person, so we set off in the general direction of NYC. I mean, I know how to get out of the state, and had a fairly good idea of which way to head once we reached Mississippi. We made it to Atlanta, Georgia by the first night and stayed with Julia's parents. (See? We were already doing good with our money) The second night was spent in Baltimore, and we spent the whole day riding the subway back and forth across town in D.C.

We were having a simply marvelous time. There were no children to cook for, no husbands to account to for our time, nobody to tell us we were spending too much time on the subway. We stayed a second night at the hotel in Baltimore, with plans to head to Atlantic City the next morning. Each of the places we'd stayed at were regular hotels where you drive up and put your suitcases inside your room while waiting for the air conditioner to regulate itself. Not so in Atlantic City.

As soon as we drove up toward the hotel, I could see porters unloading suitcases and carry bags from the trunks of cars and then driving the cars away. This is otherwise known as valet parking. Since all of my good clothes were lying in a large black plastic bag on the backseat, and since my hair care products were in Wal-Mart bags on the floor beside me (ditto for my friend), we experienced several moments of intense panic wondering how we were going to keep the porter from discovering we'd packed in plastic bags. We decided we just would tell them we had no luggage, find out where the van was parked, and then go get all of our stuff ourselves. So, that's what we told the porter: We had no luggage. He stopped and stared at us with a puzzled face, but asked no questions. Then I asked him, as casually as possible, just precisely where the van would be parked. He said they drove the vehicles a couple of miles away and kept them in a parking lot. Darn. Foiled again. I asked him to hold on a moment and went to confer with my friend. We decided we really didn't want to trek several miles with our plastic bags, so we told the porter we'd go ahead and have him bring what we had up to the room.

I imagine the porter must've thought we were insane by this point, but it only got worse when he opened the van door and several canned goods rolled out onto the ground under the covered pull-up area. See, as we drove through Philadelphia, we saw that a Save-a-Center was going out of business and all their groceries were marked way down. We'd stopped and spent a lot of our money on the groceries and put them behind us in the van. That's what fell out of the van when the porter reached for our plastic bags of clothes.

In as calm a tone as I could muster, I pointed out which of my plastic bags were to go onto the lovely brass carts carrying luggage, and which were to stay. Meanwhile, my friend was chasing down stray rolling canned goods. The porter loaded our things and proceeded to follow us into the hotel. We desperately tried to stay as far away from him as possible, lest anyone think that the things he was carting were ours. He kept following us, though.

The next morning we left for NYC. I'd looked at a map at the hotel, so I knew where we needed to go. It was thrilling driving into Manhattan. We drove around for blocks, site-seeing from the car, looking at places we'd only seen in the movies, when it became apparent that was all we were going to do. There wasn't one single parking place. Not one. We drove for a total of 4 hours, never finding a space. People were screaming obscenities at us, hollering in general, honking horns, blaring music. We knew that before we left, we had to at least buy our kids souvenirs, so we got the bright idea that if my friend let me off at the corner, I could run into a store and grab some t-shirts. Julia, meanwhile, would drive around the block and then come and pick me up. I finished shopping and waited forever for her to pick me up. She'd gotten turned around on the one-way streets and ran into streets under construction and had to wind her way back to me.

Julia never left the car the entire time we were there. I pointed out the World Trade Centers, the Statue of Liberty, the Empire State Building, Broadway, and she says she never saw any of it for fear of taking her eyes off the road. After four hours, we couldn't take any more. We left the city and pulled into the first town we could find, just to calm down and decide what to do next. Home was sounding better and better every minute. It was the best trip I ever took.

12

Nothing More Than Feelings

I walked over to mom's yesterday to see how her crape myrtles are coming along - everything bloomed very early this year due to our mild and wet winter - and I was telling her that I wanted to sit down and have a cup of coffee with her. She asked what was wrong - moms are just that way, aren't they? I said a non-committal 'oh, nothing' and mentioned that I was just feeling a little down. Then, as if she were offering a fresh-baked cookie, she asked if I wanted a tranquilizer. I must've paused a moment too long with my eyebrows raised to my hairline, because she said, "Come on, it'll relax you and make you feel better." I thought that, considering I so rarely even take cough syrup, I'd probably fall into a stupor for the rest of the day if I took one of those happy pills.

I've heard of people who have no ability to feel physical pain. I thought that perhaps it might be something wonderful to have no ability to sense pain. The article or news story, I can't remember how I came across this information, went on to explain though, that the people with this particular disorder don't know when they've hurt themselves. They could pick up a pan of scalding water and the pan wouldn't burn them. Oh, the blisters and oozing would appear, but the pain would be dulled or even non-existent. In fact, these people have to be even more careful not to hurt themselves than we do, because no pain receptors are there to warn them of danger.

And isn't that what our emotions do for us? Embarrassment reminds us that we are probably being idiots. Fear tells us to run quickly and avoid problems. Love, well, love allows us to look the other way. It also makes us stand up to our obligations and do what's right. And it gives us compassion. I have a quote taped on my computer at work which says, "Compassion isn't real compassion when it is used selectively; it becomes, instead, judgment." Don't worry, you won't have to pay at the door for that tidbit of wisdom; I threw it in for free.

So, no, I think I'll pass on dulling my emotions. They make me a good mom and a good friend. And sometimes, they let me know when I've done something truly, amazingly stupid.

13

I'm A Red-Necked Woman,
Not Some High Class Broad

I have a confession to make. For all of my lady-like ways, prissiness, and desire to wear my tiara and big hair on every conceivable appropriate occasion, there is this part of me, this woman in me, who must've been a redneck in a prior lifetime.

I have discovered, through my southern best-girlfriend, that there is such a thing as the 'Blue Collar Comedy Tour.' She told me I would love it. I was somewhat dubious, but decided to try it anyway. Trust me, sitting on the sofa with my mocha cappuccino and my non-fiction "Behind the Oscars" book (I always read and watch television at the same time), I was hardly prepared for the fun I would have watching the dvd of the comedy tour. I didn't want to laugh - it was beneath me to laugh at a joke who's punch line was, "I don't think so, Scooter" - but laugh I did. Hysterically. I was entertained enough to almost set my book down at one point.

The jokes reminded me of my growing up years and they hit close to home. But aren't those the things we laugh at the most? I don't find a lot of humor in poking fun at others, but honey darlin', poke fun at me and the folks I love, and I can't stop the tears of laughter. When I think of how many things "You might be a redneck if..." apply to me or those I know, well, I smile. A lot. There was a time when it would embarrass me for others, other more refined folks, to know I associated with 'those kind' of people, but now, I can appreciate that behind the majority of the humor, there is an entire population of determined people who, though poor, find a way to make do. Of course, one has to realize that, after the War of Northern Aggression, we were left dirt poor in this region. Folks who had plenty were reduced immediately to folks who had nothing but their smarts left to them.

I mean, who else but a southerner could come up with the ingenious device I saw in Ron's Seafood Market and Nail Care Shop the other day? It was a Redneck Daiquiri Mixer that one could take on picnics or even tailgating. The mixer consisted of a small ice chest with a garbage disposal (a NEW one!) attached to the back and connected to the ice chest with two hoses: one for sucking in and one for pushing out the daiquiri mix and ice. It was a stroke of genius! Whole huge batches of pina coladas or strawberry daiquiris could be mixed all at once. Granted, it was a little loud, but hey, after a few sips, who would care?

And really, who else but a southerner could have come up with the idea of selling live bait in vending machines right outside the K-Mart next to the cokes?

Yes, it's taken me almost 40 years to embrace this part of my southerness. Give me time, though; I'm growing and I have a long way to go. So, bless my heart, and in the spirit of those most famous last words ever uttered by a Southerner, "Hey y'all, watch this!"

14

And She'll Have Fun, Fun, Fun Till Her Daddy Takes Her T-Bird Away, ….. Or Was It a Corvette?

Is there some cosmic explanation for the weird and random strengths and weaknesses in my life? I feel that I am a fairly intelligent woman; after all, I've taught school, I have a college degree, I work for the newspaper, I used to be the director of a computer college, and icing on the cake, I've been a mom for 20 years now. Give me a blank Access program and I can write a database that will whistle and hum and do somersaults for you backwards and forwards. Give me a blank sheet of paper and I can fill it with poetry that makes sense. Hand me an empty pot and I will make you the best seafood gumbo you've ever put into your mouth, all from memory.

But ask me to name a car and I'm helpless. My best friend, Julia, is getting a new car. First, she tells me about this type of car and that type of car - she seemingly knows them all. We'll drive into the parking lot at work and she'll say, "Oh, look, Steve, Molly, and Judy are here," and I'm left turning my head this way and that trying to see my co-workers on the sidewalk. Julia can tell they're here because she knows which cars are in the parking lot. Well, I've figured out one co-worker's car, but I'll be danged if I have any clue what the others look like. I don't want to embarrass myself after all these months by asking my friends to point out which cars are theirs.

My sons can point out every make and model of car, and I'm left guessing what they're talking about. Okay, I know what a Mustang looks like because it has a horse on it, but if we drive by too fast and I don't see the horse, I'm sunk.

Which brings me to a great story. My husband was working on his car. He was elbow deep in grease and muck and had pulled off the radiator. The thing was full of rust or holes or some other nastiness, and he needed me to take it to the radiator place so they could fix it. So, I hopped in my car (the small blue one) and drove 25 minutes into town. I arrived at the mechanic's garage and had to wait in the lobby for a little while. I flipped through magazines (Women's Fitness, go figure) and finally it was my turn. I went out into the greasy garage and the young guy was standing there holding the radiator.

I thought, "Oh, good, he's already got it fixed." Then he said, "Lady, I cain't fix this here thang. It's plumb full o' holes. Ya gonna hafta get a new one." Well, I had the checkbook with me and thought this couldn't be too hard. Then he asked, "What kinda car'd this come off of anyway? I got lots of 'em in stock." I panicked. I stood there for a moment and hemmed and hawed and he asked me again, "This yer husband's car, Ma'am? What kind is it?" I swear to Moses, I could not think of what kind of car he had. I don't know that I ever knew what kind of car he had. I always referred to it as 'your blue car,' you know, as opposed to 'my blue car.' So, I answered, "Um, blue?" He stopped for a second and cocked his head. Then he started to laugh. He said, "Dang lady, don'tcha know yer own car?"

I tried calling my husband, but since he was outside, he couldn't hear the phone ringing. I stayed there 20 minutes trying to call him. Finally he answered and I was able to ask. He laughed and laughed, figuring, I suppose, that I'd known for years what sort of car it was. He was mistaken.

I wish I could say I've gotten better, but the truth is, I guess cars are just a fact that my brain doesn't register as knowledge to remember. If a car runs, I'm happy. Oh, yeah, the car was a ..... Sunbird? Is that a type of car? Maybe it was a Saturn. It was something that started with an S. I do recall it was blue......

15

Time Keeps On Slippin'

This morning I tore off June from my main wall calendar at my desk. I expect that sometime after my birthday on the 6th next month, I'll get around to viewing August.

Don't get me wrong, I live by deadlines and dates, but I have to keep them in my head, because even when I meticulously write them down on the calendar, I forget to look at the calendar, or I lose it, or it gets covered up, or stuff spills on it, or I doodle all over it to the point of obliteration, or... whatever. I've been given beautiful day-planners on several occasions as gifts. One year, I opened the brand-spanking-new day-planner and wrote, "Pick up Thomas' bicycle" on a fresh calendar page in January. Months later when I found the planner again, I opened it to see that lone entry. I think I picked up the bicycle, but I don't know if it was on the correct day or not.

There are things at work that I have to keep up with in order to keep them scheduled. I keep a record online of when my ads run, so I don't need a calendar for that. I leave post-it notes directly on my computer screen if there's something I absolutely have to remember for the next day. I will e-mail myself things from the house that I need to do at work, and vice versa. Often times in the evening, I'll call myself at work and leave a message like this: "Evelyn, this is Evelyn. Please remember to go upstairs and pick up the insert orders tomorrow morning from Creative Services. Thank you and I sure hope you have a wonderful day today. Bye!" When I get to work the next morning, I'm always so excited to see that I have a voice mail and end up laughing because the voice mail is from me.

Unfortunately, this method does not always work. Several years ago, I planned a "Home Interiors" party where women get together and shop from catalogs while viewing merchandise brought in by a Home Interiors salesperson. I planned this party for weeks, sent out invitations, ordered food to be delivered, etc. My girlfriend said we could have it at her house since her house was bigger than mine. The big day arrived and I got dressed and all dolled-up for the event. Then I started cooking supper. The guys came home from school and I served supper to them, making myself a plate at the same time. I sat down and started eating with them and when we were all done, I started cleaning the kitchen.

As I was loading the dishwasher, my friend called and said, "Um, everyone is here and we went ahead and started without you. Are you coming tonight or what?" I was standing there wearing the high heels I'd put on in order to go to my own party and had forgotten to leave the house. I showed up 45 minutes late for a party I was hosting. What a doofus. I wish I could say that was the last major event I forgot to attend, but alas, it is not.

It's already July 10. I know this solely because I just glanced up at the date. Where has this year gone? I know, I know, if I kept a working calendar....

16

I Went Sky Diving, I Went Rocky Mountain Climbing

Well, not exactly, and I didn't ride 2.7 seconds on a bull named Fu-Manchu, either. But I did paint a door red, and that has to count for something, does it not?

When I was in my mid-20s, before I discovered that there was such a creature as high-end perfume (having been an Avon-type gal myself), my mother-in-law bought herself an Elizabeth Arden perfume named "Red Door." The box was, obviously, made in the shape of a bright, scarlet red door. I was enamored instantly with both the perfume, of which I have a bottle even now, and the Red Door. That's how I always think of it in my mind: a capital R and a capital D. And thus a dream of mine began to take shape. I wanted a Red Door.

This may not appear to be much to you, gentle reader, however for me, a Red Door epitomized something exciting, daring, zippy, and irrationally extravagant. Not everyone is a Red Door-type person. In fact, many people considered this a zany idea. I mean, why a Red Door, for heaven's sake, asked my mother with a smirky scowl on her face.

At my last house, a lovely, creamy yellow and white confection of color, a Red Door would have simply been horrendous. Still the dream lived on. Until yesterday, when, after a long and exhausting search for the perfect exterior door paint shade of Red, I happened upon a spicy Fire Engine blaze of color. It came home with me. I decided not to paint the doors on my house, but to paint my shed/cottage doors instead. Ok, I'm brave, but not quite brave enough to actually put this color on my actual house.

So, off came the doors. I began painting at 12 noon, albeit in a spot of shade. And I painted. And painted. And painted some more. For those of you uninitiated in the painting of the color Red, allow me a moment to enlighten you. One does not merely choose to paint the color Red; one makes a commitment to painting the color Red. This is a long-term commitment, because once you start, there's no going back until you've painted at least 5 to 6 coats. I was experienced with this already, being that my kitchen is a lovely version of Tomato Spice Red. I committed to painting the kitchen for three days, layer after shiny layer. I knew what I was in store for with the doors and I was not disappointed. Five hours later, after four coats on both sides, I declared myself finished. My hand is now a useless stump, but by-cracky, I have Red Doors. One dream down, a million to go.

On a roll, I decided to realize yet another dream of mine: having a microwave oven that matched the rest of my kitchen, without actually having to purchase a new one.

My microwave oven is almost 18 years old, and unlike my other stainless steel kitchen appliances, my microwave is white. I wanted it black, since I really don't know how to paint things a stainless steel color. So, while buying Red paint, I grabbed a can of black appliance paint, too. I cleaned the microwave, took it outside, carefully taped off the door and plug and carefully painted the oven. All was well. Then I came inside to watch television while the paint dried.

About an hour later, I went outside to survey my painted work of art. I noticed something odd as I approached - the microwave seemed to be moving all on itself. I walked up and realized that it was covered with ants. OHMYGOD. They were in the casing, on the motor, inside the oven where it cooks, everywhere. I picked up the oven and dropped it a bunch of times, getting bitten and probably breaking it in the process and for sure scratching up my paint job in a terrible way. I grabbed ant spray and killed all the little monsters, but that oven stayed outside on the driveway until I knew every last one of them was dead. At least the Red Door came out okay.

17

Uptown Girl

It was about time. For the past 41 years of my life, which, ironically, are all the years I've been alive, I've not lived in a home that had cable. I've had dial-up access for my computer, and on the television, I've had the 4 major channels that my trusty little antenna could provide. While others watched the exciting "Trading Spaces," I was left with LPB's "This Old House." Not quite the same, although I have learned a lot about dovetailing and biscuits and hardwoods over the years. I would listen with envy when friends of mine would regale me, as recently as this week, with exotic titles such as "Six Feet Under." What the heck is that? Sounds cool.

Even better, my old dial-up connection is now a dinosaur of my past. There have been a few difficulties along the way, though. Yesterday afternoon, I was zipping along, viewing this video, listening to that music, chatting on messenger and in general, having a grand ol' time. My husband came home then with a wireless router for his laptop so that we could share the cable internet. This sounded like a lovely idea. That idea quickly disintegrated into bitterly shattered dreams and ambitions. He connected everything, ran the set up disk, and instantly, my yahoo messenger went away. HOLY BAD CONNECTIONS, BATMAN!!!! This was not a good thing. I stomped, I fussed, I fumed, I uninstalled and reinstalled yahoo messenger a grand total of three complete times and still nothing. And then, JesusMaryandJoseph, my entire internet connection on my computer went away. Oh, sure, my husband's laptop was whiz-banging its way through the internet like lightning, while I got "work offline?" prompts.

Eventually, probably through no help on my part, although I was offering novenas and Hail Mary's on its behalf, my computer entered into peace talks with the wireless router, and by 11:30 pm, my internet and my messenger were back in business.

It seems though, that some of us are just never satisfied. My youngest son came into my office and whined, "How come there's not more kid's channels???" I prepared myself for the big speech - "Look son, back when I was walking through snow to school and back, I lived for 40 years with no cable at all........"

18

Love, Sweet Love

I adore surprises and presents - big ones, small ones, sparkly ones, thoughtful ones, unthoughtful ones, ones that go whiz or bang or spray whipped cream, ones that sit there and look beautiful, ones that serve a purpose, and ones that serve no useful purpose whatsoever. But what I really, really love, more than anything in the world, are gifts of words. Poetry, letters, short or long messages, jotted notes... no matter, they all find a way into my heart. On the flip side, harsh and cold words will cut and wound and scar me deeply, and usually for a long time.

Now, my husband doesn't like gifts at all, and frankly, wouldn't care if he never received another one. But man, oh, man, what he loves is when

I do something nice for him, or better, when I run an errand for him. If I put gas in my car, he's happy. If I take his truck and put gas in it, he's ecstatic, and if I call the insurance company to find out why they haven't paid the doctor yet, he's downright euphoric. To him, these little gifts or acts of service make him feel loved.

This past week, I asked him if he'd like anything special for Father's Day. He asked for some time to think about it. Later on, he came back and said, "You know, what I really want is for you to make me a big pot of your spaghetti." I just stared at him. He was serious. The man is insane for my spaghetti, and who could blame him, but this is the only present he wanted for Fathers Day. May I say, and I do, that I made the best pot of spaghetti I have ever produced. Mmmm.... full of onions, peppers, mushrooms of all shapes and sizes, sweet Italian sausages, small and soft meatballs, everything all hot and spicy and sweet and tangy. (It doesn't take much to get me off topic, does it?) Suffice it to say, he was so happy to get his spaghetti, and considering the time I spent on it, it really was a labor of love.

A number of years ago, I read a book by Gary Chapman called, "The Five Love Languages." Though I understood the concept, I'd never really put it all together in my mind. The premise goes something like this: Everyone has a language in which they understand, give, and receive love. For some people, spending time with them really makes them feel loved. For others, sweet and kind words of affirmation send them soaring. For others, performing small, loving acts help them know they are loved. Still others need physical touch to feel acceptance. Receiving presents is the greatest thing in the world for some folks. If you can figure out the way someone in your life receives love, and you can love them that way, they will see and sense your caring and affection.

For years, I would tell my husband, "You don't make me feel loved." I said this because it was true. Did it mean he didn't love me? No, not at all. He just didn't know how to love me in a way I could see it. He says that he felt helpless when I'd say this. I have to admit, many times, he still does. I tried to explain that I needed words, tender words, words of affirmation, to make me feel loved. I didn't care if he filled my car with gas; I wanted to hear that I was beautiful, smart, a good mom, a good friend, and I wanted sweet notes and pretty cards and letters. I needed them. Need them. To him, however, putting gas in my car was his way of saying 'I love you.'

Why do I find it difficult sometimes to pinpoint the way those close to me will feel my immense love for them? I will admit that at times, I fail at showing others love in the way they need to receive it; yet, when I do, the rewards are phenomenal. All the world needs is love, sweet love. Give some.

19

I Scream, You Scream, We All Scream

It was decided that today of all days was going to be a Baskin-Robbins Day. I went in and asked for a double-scoop sundae. I was craving Nutty Coconut and Truffle In Paradise with hot fudge. I paid for my treat and walked out to my car. That's when I noticed I didn't have hot fudge. So, I got out of the car and walked back in. "I would REALLY like my hot fudge, please." The man put it all on top of my whipped cream, thus melting it into a puddle. Sigh.

After driving out of the parking lot, I moved the ice cream around in the cup looking for my white Nutty Coconut scoop. Nothing. I pulled back into the lot and walked inside, placing my cup on the counter. "Sir, there is no Nutty Coconut in this cup. I am not trying to be a problem, but I have had a bad day and I. Want. My. Two. Scoops. Of. Ice cream. The. Way. I. Ordered. Them." He took my cup and kept furtively cutting his eyes toward me while I waited.

As I was leaving, the manager said, "Ma'am, I'm sorry, but this guy is new - he's only been here three days now." As God is my witness, it took all of my willpower to not turn back and shout: AND HOW MANY DAYS DOES IT TAKE TO LEARN HOW TO COUNT TO TWO?!? Thankfully, I kept myself in check, smiled sweetly, and said, "Well, bless his heart."

20

Bit By Bit, Putting It Together

Embarrassing as it may be, I have to admit that one year ago, I began knitting a scarf. It was all the rage last year; everyone was doing it. Considering that I will rarely consult a map when going places, it only stood to reason that I would receive the minimal training necessary to undertake such a Martha-esque endeavor. My teacher gave me less than 7 minutes of instruction before going out of town. I neglected to learn important things like counting stitches on each line so that your scarf doesn't grow wider with each row, totaling 12 inches across when you're halfway through. Or, such as, in an effort to make perfect little uniform stitches, not making them so tight that you could use the scarf as a thermal blanket when you're through. Yeah, those things would have been nice to know.

So, once I reached 12 inches wide and 48 inches long (it started as 4 inches wide), I put the scarf down in disgust, knowing it would never touch my body and that it was too ugly to give someone as a gift, unless it was somebody I really hated bad. I put my knitting needles and all my beautiful, silky yarn on the sewing counter in my office and watched it for one long year. I have felt so guilty. Part of the reason I wouldn't do anything with it is because I knew I was going to have to take out every stitch and start over.

It's taken a year to do what I knew needed to be done. I carefully pulled all the yarn apart and rolled it into a ball. There must be 2 pounds of yarn there; enough to knit a blanket for medium-sized child. I honestly felt tremendous relief upon seeing it all rolled-up. It became a blank canvas all over again.

Of course, the first afternoon when I was determined to do it on my own with no additional instructions, I sat through three hours of mind-numbing television while trying to figure out the stitches. I was convinced that, just like a song will come back to you on the piano, surely the stitches would come back to me. Alas, they did not. I found a nice instruction site online and slowly began that first row casting on, then the next row, casting off. I did this so many times, I was ready to 'cast-off' the whole thing before my rhythm and movement became fluid. And bit by bit, piece by piece, I began putting it together.

We don't always get a clean slate with everything in our lives. I know that I have made some dreadful mistakes in many areas and at many different times in my life, and unfortunately, I know if given the chance again, I'd probably do things the same way. I know me. However, on that rare occasion when I have the opportunity to wipe the slate clean and start again, there's almost a feeling of rebirth, and I don't take that lightly.

I'm almost through now with my scarf. My stitches are loopy and soft, each row with the correct number cast on and off, and I am so proud of myself. I'm thinking that possibly my friends and family members would love a soft, thin, long scarf this winter. Heavens knows I have enough yarn left over.

21

When the Moon Hits Your Eye Like a Big Pizza Pie

I've always been very proud of my Italian background; however, since my mother never had much to do with her Italian family, I never really knew that much about this part of my heritage. That does seem to be a recurring theme in my life, does it not? In order to remedy the situation, this summer I spent some quality time in the Williams Research Center on Conti St. in the French Quarter. I approached my search with some trepidation, not knowing what I would find, and not really knowing how to begin.

I spoke to the very nice woman behind the help desk at the research center and she explained how I would begin the search to find my history. First she needed to know if I knew how long ago my people came to America. I only knew that it was sometime after the Civil War since I'd heard my grandfather say that he was a second generation American. First I looked through all the immigration records (thank goodness they were alphabetized!) and found a number of Calamias who emigrated from Palermo, Sicily. I then cross-referenced those dates against the ship manifests from the Port of New York and the Port of New Orleans. Pay dirt!!!

Tomasso Joseph Calamia, my great-great grandfather traveled to America with a small child named Geralamo Calamia aboard the SS Star of India on January 3, 1890. We don't know who this child is. Perhaps a nephew or cousin? What we do know is that Tomasso settled in the French Quarter and began raising a family. He married Mary Titoro and their son was my great-grandfather Nat - short for Anatole.

I named my son Thomas Joseph after my dear grandfather, never having any idea that I'd also given him the name of our very first Calamia immigrant to America.

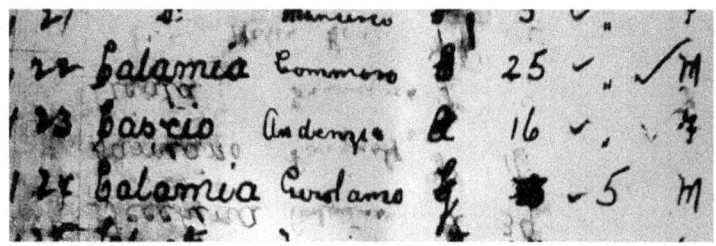

My ancestor's signature on the ship's manifest.

22

It's The Most Wonderful Time of the Year

For me, fall has always been the happiest time of all the seasons. All the best smells on earth find their way to me during these months; pumpkin pies baking, mulling spices mulling, fires burning outside, and what's better than crisp dark apples with whole cloves pressed into them? The prettiest colors come out at this time, too, and I take great pleasure in setting out pumpkins and enormous pots of colorful mums.

However, Momma said it best the other day when she hollered from her side porch, "Felt like gumbo weather this morning, didn't it?" Mind you, there's no specific day of the year set aside for making that first pot of gumbo; you have to 'feel' it. Usually that first crisp September morning sets things in motion for me.

At the end of every summer, I start gathering up the ingredients for that favorite meal of every southern Louisianan. I can remember from childhood momma telling dad as he left for work that she'd be making gumbo that day. Those were magic words. It's almost a rite of passage each year. Fresh okra is cut up and frozen, hot andouille sausage is found, plump chicken thighs are bought in bulk and the trinity (peppers, onions, celery) is cut up and ready to go.

Yesterday morning, I started my roux while it was still in the cool of the morning. I like to cook it to a dark chocolaty brown since I love the nutty flavor it gives. For someone like me who enjoys doing things in a hurry, roux is an exercise in patience. It gives me a long time to stand there and ponder the year past and the year coming up. A lot's happened this year, so this time, there's much to ponder. Maybe I should have been Jewish - they celebrate their New Year around this time, too.

So, you're all invited. Supper's on me - somebody bring the french bread, somebody bring some banana pudding, I'll have the potato salad and the gumbo's on the stove. Y'all come now!

23

Put Your Behind in Your Past

"Giving up hope for a better past." I came across that thought recently and it has haunted me since. My past. It's filled with some serious disappointments and some things that no children should have to bear in their memories. Part of the reason I began writing was to find a way to 'let go' of some of the more hurtful memories. I had hoped that by seeing black letters on white paper I would be able to disassociate myself from the scenes that play themselves out in my mind. And true, to a degree, it has helped.

Still, these words fill my mind: giving up hope for a better past. Do we actually 'choose' to let go of things that hurt us? Okay.... hurt 'me'?

And how far back do I have to go? Are we talking about all the way back to childhood, or should I really just also let go of the irritation I still have about the intellectually-challenged ice cream guy at Baskin Robbins that couldn't get my order right a few weeks ago? (I haven't been back since and I'm starting to have those 'Nutty Coconut' cravings again.)

How much time have I wasted in my life sitting around wondering why my past wasn't different or better than it was? Too much.

24

I See It in Your Eyes, Maybe It Was Better Left Unsaid

Twenty-two years ago, I met this really great guy. He was quite handsome, he was very smart, he was a hard worker, and he was good. Most of all, he met my criteria for having a name that started with a 'D.' All my boyfriends had names that started with D's (David N., David H., Darryl B., Darren B.) and the new guy was no exception: Dennis. We dated for four years, all the way through college, and then we were married.

Life went on with our marriage being probably not much different than a lot of marriages, which means that, after children and life interfered, we each existed in our own world, occasionally coming together for an argument. Eventually, at year 15, we separated. Most of the reasons circled around me leaving our church. Religion can do strange things to people's perspectives at times.

During our separation, my husband began to change – truly change. He later said that it's amazing the clarity that comes when you are alone staring at the ceiling at 4 a.m. We got together again a couple of months later and finished the house we'd started building before the separation. (In my opinion, building a second house would destroy anybody's marriage.)

We began learning new ways to communicate and most of our 'discussions' have ended peacefully. Until two nights ago. Let me tell you, there was a knock-down drag-out the likes of which you've never seen. Man, we brought his mom and dad, my mom and dad, Jesus, the cats, the neighbors, homework, housework, and the kitchen sink into that fight. I said things I would never dream of saying and he outdid me two to one.

And then, right in the middle of it all, without knocking, my youngest son Benjamin walked into our bedroom and handed my husband and I each a sheet of paper on which he had written, "Dear Mom (Dad), I love you so much. I hope I didn't do anything to make you so angry. You are the best Mom (Dad) EVER. Love, Benjamin." Well, that stopped us in our tracks. I don't know how we thought the kids hadn't heard us downstairs in their rooms. Unfortunately, in the midst of my shame, I was still angry because of the fight itself.

I look back on that evening with a lot of shame. I'm the wife who brings flowers to her husband, who cooks and cleans and tries to make his life easier. I'm the woman who would almost never say an unkind thing to someone even if they deserved it. And yet, I lost my mind apparently, and tore my husband to shreds. Sadly, I unwittingly also scared my children to death, and for that, I have no excuse.

I felt awful after the fight. I wanted to reach out and grab all the unkind words I'd said and make them disappear. Of course, I apologized through tears and did all that I could to make it better. When will I learn my lesson? We are taught today that we should speak our minds, say everything that's in our hearts, and get it off our chest. I don't think, though, that this is always the best advice. Somethings are better left unsaid, while "be ye kind one to another" is the better route to take.

25

When I Was Young, I'd Listen to the Radio

Turn on music, and you'll find me instantly transported back in time the second a certain song comes on the radio.

"She's a brick house, she's mighty mighty just lettin' it all hang out." Wow. What a fun song! I'm brought back to simpler times in jr. high when I wore bell-bottomed pants, ponchos, glasses and frizzy hair. We'd listen to music in the common area at school, and I remember the girls giggling when that song would come on and the boys would pretend that they were singing the words. Some of the girls would dance to a few lines trying to draw attention from the guys. Not me; I was too shy, but I laughed nonetheless. Even just typing the words brings a big smile to my face.

Or maybe I'm transported back to a dark and dreamy night dancing with my guy too many years ago to count as I recall with fondness the butterflies-in-the-tummy feeling I had. "I've looked at life from both sides now, from give and take and still somehow, it's life's illusions I recall – I really don't know life at all." Slow and quiet. Peaceful. Loving. I'll remember that evening as long as I live and a part of me belongs to that moment in time. I was in love as deeply and passionately as only those who give of themselves utterly can know. We danced so gently, we almost didn't dance at all.

"Sentimental gentle winds, blowing through my life again, sentimental lady, gentle one." I only associate deep sadness with this song. I remember well the slanted sunlight on the face of one I cared for as I said good-bye. I remember closing my eyes and feeling tears hot on my cheeks and I can hear him singing softly to me with the song on the radio. So long ago. How can it still affect me this profoundly?

I absolutely cannot forget the night I danced for the last time when I was young. I didn't know it at the time, but it would be years before I was to dance again. My date and I were at an old gymnasium/roller rink sort of place and there had to be hundreds of teenagers gathered together all the way out in the boondocks. It was dark and hot and the music was ear-blasting loud. "You dropped a bomb on me, baby! You dropped a bomb on me!" 1984. I was happy and wildly carefree that night. We danced hard for hours. I remember standing in line forever for a coke and when a new song would start, we'd abandon the line just to dance again.

I often wonder which songs I will look back on in a few years. Which songs will I define certain times with? Which ones will bring me happy memories or sad? I'm looking forward to finding out.

26

Are You Going To Scarborough Fair?

A brilliant era has come to end. Today I discovered I am no longer as carefree and wild as previously thought. Thought by me, at least.

Fairs have always held a wonderful attraction for me. The sounds and smells bring me to a natural emotional high like none other. I love cotton candy, enjoying the look of it as much or more than the sticky-sweet taste, and I love both caramel and candied apples. Of course, if you look long enough, somebody somewhere is going to be deep-frying something, whether it's a Twinkie or a Snickers bar. Hey, don't knock the Snickers-on-a-stick; it's pure heaven. My usual poison of choice is a funnel cake, disguised as a mound of powdered sugar.

Every sense is awakened at a fair. The smell of peanuts roasting is a favorite of mine, as is the smell of barbeque, scents that go as far back as my memory. Children scream and laugh, barkers call you to see the Fat Lady or the 5-legged calf and calliopes play bright, carnival sounds. Blinding neon lights flash on every ride, beckoning normal people into defying death as they swing and swish and dip and glide and scream their lungs out.

Which brings me to what became a terribly poignant moment today. Today I stood and watched as my sons and husband rode things that spin faster than my washing machine on the rinse cycle. Ben and his little friend rode the Bullet, a fantastical device that careens toward the earth, well, like a bullet. And I stood and watched, knowing that if I got onto even one of them, I would embarrass myself by spraying the crowd with undigested funnel cake.

It's not always been like this. I have fond memories of Six Flags Over Texas where I rode the Drop thing again and again - plunging straight down from 11 stories in the air. WOW. I've always loved the big cage that spins everyone so fast, you can pick your feet up off the floor and still remain plastered to the inside of the basket. And I would ride these over and over, as fast as the operator would let me get back in line. Not so anymore. In the immortal words of Wendy, "I've become old, Peter; I am ever so much more than twenty."

Today was not a complete wash, though. Since it was a fair being hosted by Ben's school, I was one of the parents asked to man (or woman) a booth this morning. I volunteered Thomas to help me, and we were assigned to a Fishing Booth for small-ish children. The object was for the kiddo to put his hook over our Wall of Water and snag a Really Big Prize. The children didn't know that Thomas was behind the Wall of Water clipping small bags of prizes onto the fishing line with clothespins.

Thomas, always looking for a fun way to do a rather boring task, discovered that if he held onto the fishing line tightly as the children desperately tried to raise their prize up into the air, he could let go at the right moment and the spring-loaded rod would snap the prize straight up and over the Wall of Water. He further discovered that if he aimed correctly, he could bean the little kid with the small bag. After six kids got hit, I made him stop. Actually, it was only when a stray flying bag hit a passing woman that I made him stop. She looked at me as if *I* had done it, so that was the end of his fun.

I'm thinking next year I'll try a ride before the funnel cake. Maybe that's the trick. If not, then I'm taking over the Jolly Roger Choo-Choo Train, and all those three year-olds can just wait their turn.

27

Birds Do It, Bees Do It, Even Monkeys in the Trees Do It

"Wow. I just can't believe freckles can do all that."

My older son had spoken these words to me as we were taking a short road trip. I've tried to spend a fair amount of one-on-one time with each of my sons, always telling them that they could talk to me about anything.

This particular trip was set aside as a time to finally tell my son about the birds and the bees. He was 11 years old and had asked me how babies are made. I always knew I'd be the parent who ended up talking to the boys, as my husband had been content to let them find out about life on their own. On the other hand, I wanted my sons to freely discuss any questions they had with me. I was the liberated parent. I was the scared parent.

I sat for a full minute after my son mentioned the freckles. I looked over at him as he peered intently at the dark freckles on his arms, running his fingers across the raised bumps.

"Yeah, mom, I just can't believe freckles can do all that."

I'd spent the last 30 minutes describing to my son just exactly how babies are made. Freckles? Somewhere I'd gone terribly wrong in my explanation. I went back over the conversation in my mind....

"Well, son, um, uh... well, now, you know those small, round balls between your legs? You know, your testicles? Well, they uh, they make what essentially is fertilizer for the eggs that a woman's body makes. Do you understand so far?"

"Uh-huh."

"And uh, then, um, that fertilizer, it's um, it's called, uh, sperm. And, well, that sperm meets up with the woman's body inside her, and uh, uh, well, um, she has eggs inside her body and the sperm fertilizes those eggs. Inside her."

We'd gone on like this for 20 minutes or more, all the while I was trying to find the courage to say words I never say aloud. And now my son had the impression that freckles were responsible for this great feat.

"Now, I'm not exactly sure what you mean, son. I'm not sure what you mean by freckles."

"Well, you told me that small, brown balls on my legs, you know, my FRECKLES, made the fertilizer for a woman's eggs."

I had to stop the car. I could not let my son see that I was about to fall over laughing.

"No, sweetheart, I said testicles, not freckles."

He sat there awhile pondering this new information. I had my hand across my mouth, looking out the car window and away from my son.

He chuckled, "I knew freckles couldn't do all that."

28

It's a Beautiful Ride

When I was a very young adult, like every other person, I had dreams and ambitions of what my life would be like. I would live in a nice little village-type town with my friends and family surrounding me, and though it sounds cliché, I wanted a pristine white picket fence with lavender wisteria growing up and around an arbor near the front door. Enormous pink roses would follow trellises and my porch would have a large wicker swing with the requisite creak, creak, creak as the chains it hung upon moved against the hooks.

My husband would always be thoughtful and bring me flowers and spin me around and break into a huge smile when he saw me, and I would wear beautiful cotton dresses and hats with ribbons as I gathered herbs for supper.

Somehow, I never managed to fill in the 'reality' details of this picture-perfect dream I had. I just knew life would be beautiful. And so it has been.

Though that man I married doesn't spin me around or always break into a big smile, he is the hardest working man I know. He's paid every bill on time from the day we were married. I, on the other hand, don't even know where the bills are.

My older son isn't a Math or English whiz, and he has to fight for every good grade he gets, but he is musically gifted beyond description. Is he perfect? No, but he is more than I ever dreamed possible in a child. He is my best friend.

My youngest son gave me fits when he was little, but inside that passionate child was the most tender, compassionate and giving person I know. His unselfishness puts me to shame every day of my life.

It's funny how the trivial things of life melt away especially during this time of year. The friendship of those around me and the love of those closest to me become the only things that matter.

Oh, and that swing? It's on my back porch. And life? It's beautiful.

The three handsome men in my life.

29

Painted Candy Canes on the Tree

For many of us, there are no greater memories than those we have of the holidays. I'd like to share a few of mine with you. In 1985 I was 19 years old and of an extremely curious nature.

I'd just left snowy Chicago to come home for the Christmas holidays, and Louisiana had the same bone-chilling, wet cold. Momma had left a hose dribbling to keep the pipes from freezing, and I'd spent the better part of the day looking at that magnificent little blob of ice that had formed at the end of the hose. For all I knew, Whoville could be located in that small icy Wonderland.

My sister and brother and I spent the other part of the day learning the rest of the words to Elvis' "Blue Christmas." I was the self-imposed Entertainment Hostess, and I had it set in my head that we were going to perform for my parents the night before we opened presents. I did, and still do, a mean Elvis impersonation, and Becky and Charlie were my back-up do-wap singers. Charlie couldn't keep rhythm and eventually wandered off after I insulted his arm-waving and snapping abilities. Okay, so he was only five. I should have been more patient.

My parents were not wealthy. That's the polite way of saying we were quite poor. Every year before Christmas, they would sit us down and ask our forgiveness for them not being able to give us good presents, but somehow, we always felt very rich after Santa came. My two favorite years were when I received a child-sized telescope, and the time I got a Miss America Barbie and a Barbie Carousel Kitchen. OHMYGOSH!! The carousel kitchen would spin around when Barbie would stand on the button. The sink had tiny dishes and the cabinets were filled with thimble-sized canned goods, and if you slid the lever just right, the oven would shine red inside when you put the tiny plastic turkey in it.

Once I reached the age where no one believed in Santa (I have since changed my opinion, by the way), I began searching each year for my presents. Even though I was never dumb enough to confess, I think my mother knew I'd go looking, because every year, the hiding place changed. This particular year, I hadn't been able to find my presents at all and I was getting desperate.

By now, all the presents were wrapped and under the tree. My parents went to bed early every night due to dad's work schedule, and I was often up alone. I had never done anything so brave as actually opening a wrapped gift, but that night, I could no longer stand just seeing those tantalizingly shiny boxes under our tree. I waited until everyone had been asleep for at least an hour.

At first, I just held the boxes with my name on them. The shaking and waving came later, my hunger-to-know growing with each thunk and jingle inside the box. Momma always situated our tree in a corner of the living room and waaaay in the back under the tree limbs, I could see one more present that looked like it might have an E-V-E-L-Y-N on the tag. I scooted all the way as close to the wall as I could get and I still couldn't reach that box. I stuck my leg under the tree - nothing. I was going to have to dive for it.

I carefully moved all the other boxes out of the way and began belly-crawling to the back of the tree. So far, so good. And I hit pay dirt - the present was for me! Very carefully, I scooted back out from the tree, my present tightly gripped. OWWW! Ouch!! My naturally curly longish hair became tangled in the lowest branch. I moved, I wiggled, I fought, to no avail. And then I pulled. Harder. Harder still.... and then, as if in slow motion, that gigantic-to-a-small-girl tree fell over on top of my prone body.

I probably laid there a full minute trying to not panic and trying not to cry - the branches and needles were stabbing me everywhere. I rolled out from under the tree and knew instantly that I could never lift it back up on my own. Ornaments had rolled to the four corners of the room and the angel looked like a beaten and disheveled homeless woman. Needing help, I was able to eventually wake my sister, who at one point hit me right in the head as she pulled her covers up tighter, told me I was lying, and rolled over to go back to sleep.

The next morning, I could see momma eye-balling that tree, knowing that there was 'something' different about the placement of the ornaments, but not quite being able to put her finger on it.

I wish I could say that as the years passed, I was able to change my gift-seeking ways, but alas, I would be remiss. After I'd been married a few years, my husband, wise to my ways, stopped leaving presents for me under our little Charlie-Brown-homely tree. Until this one particular day. He wrapped up a small box, put it under the tree and left for work. He smiled at me so big, as though he were so proud of himself for getting me something before the 24th.

All I could think of was that he must be really stupid if he thought I wouldn't look. He wasn't gone 5 minutes before I had expertly removed the tape from the paper and opened the box. And when I gazed inside, I saw what he'd left for me. It was a note which read: "Gotcha." I was shocked. I was stunned. I laughed. It moved me, People. But I had a dilemma. If I called him to tell him, he'd know I'd opened it, and God himself knew I could never keep a secret that big.

Not one more minute passed before we were both laughing hysterically on the phone.

God bless us everyone!

30

Tiny Tots With Their Eyes All Aglow

I've recently been hearing about a new Christmas trend where giving a gift is seen as unnecessary and wasteful. Someone chided me for even giving to my own children. However, it was only when I saw the pureness and innocence of my children's faces as they could barely wait to give me a gift, that I understood the 'spirit' of Christmas. It is that same spirit which lives in those who love to give all year long, and not just during the holidays. To deny my children the ability to give to me would be to douse their warm hearts with ice water.

I cannot find it in myself to give them nothing. I see small things all year long that I know would make them smile and feel loved and thought of. I'm the same way with my husband and friends. I remember my first

Christmas with my husband. He gave me a small fluorescent light fixture for the space above my kitchen sink so I could see to wash dishes easier. Okay, at the time I was bewildered, but now I think back fondly on his thoughtfulness. He had it right. He'd thought of me and he was so proud of his gift.

Stores and Wall Street have reduced Christmas to numbers, but we don't have to live our lives that way. We teach our children to give all year. We teach them by adopting those less fortunate, by getting together warm and beautiful robes and slippers for the ladies at the battered women's shelter, and by getting needed things for the poor. The spirit of Christmas isn't a season. It's a lifestyle.

The author at four years-old.

31

I Saw Mommy Kissing Santa Claus
And Other Parental Delusions

While sitting in my lowly cubicle at work yesterday, my phone rang. I could tell from the caller ID that my mother was on the line. I was busy and almost sent it to voicemail, then thought better of it.

"Well, hello momma."

"Hey, Ev. I just wanted to call to see what you're wearing to my house Sunday night for the Christmas party." This is the Christmas party consisting of mom and dad, Dennis and me and our two kids, and my Aunt Phyllis and Uncle Benny.

"I don't know, momma. Haven't really thought about it."

"Well, I'm DRESSING UP and I don't want to be the only person dressed nice. Do you want to borrow something of mine so you can dress up?"

"Um, no, I'm fairly certain I have something nice."

"Oh, and another thing, what's a Uva Ring?"

"A what?"

"A Uva Ring. You know, for birth control, I think." I'm rolling my eyes off the top of my head at this point.

"Well, um, yes, you use it for birth control. I think your doctor has to prescribe it and then, you know, insert it."

"You have to do that EVERY TIME???"

"Mom, you can't possibly need birth control - why are you worried about this?"

"Well, it just looked so big on television, and I can't figure out what you'd do with it." My two co-workers are leaning over the edge of our cubicle walls by this point, staring at me.

"I don't know, mom. Maybe the doctor just scrunches it all up and shoves it up there. It's got medicine on it and it gradually releases it, I think. WHY are you asking me this???"

"Well, your father and I keep seeing these commercials and haven't the vaguest idea of how one is used."

"Okay, mom, well, I need to..."

"But have you ever used one?"

"Mom, I..."

"Okay, well, I have to go. Don't forget to try and wear something nice."

32

Life Is a Highway

"SweetMaryMotherOfGodAndEveryOtherSaintIKnow!"

Those were the words screaming in my head yesterday afternoon as my oldest son Thomas drove me around Baton Rouge. I've put off his license for as long as I can, citing the fact that it was my job to make sure he made it alive to his 18th birthday. He'll be 17 this spring, so it was high time for driving school. Yes, it was costly; however, after figuring in the price of raised insurance rates and a damaged car, I decided that it was more cost effective to let him learn [translated: **wreck**] on someone else's car.

I felt pretty good about my performance, because, after all, it is all about being able to tell your friends how your mom freaked out and started screaming and waving her arms. I'd managed to sit rather calmly, only reaching across to turn the steering wheel farther when it appeared that we were careening into oncoming traffic. I didn't even turn red in the face or bust a lung screaming. He says I kept my foot on the imaginary brake, but I think I only pressed it about 10 times before we got to the end of our driveway.

This whole process of letting him go has been hard. Oh, I expected it at 18. I had it planned. That's when I would "let go." Officially. So, it's been difficult this year watching him prefer to be other places than our house. What gives? Isn't our sofa just like his girlfriend's sofa? "But mom! They have Bose Surround Sound in the living room!!!" To my technologically-gifted son, this is pretty high cotton stuff.

The week after I turned 18, I went up to my mom and said that I'd be leaving home for good that afternoon. I didn't have a vehicle, I had only an offer from my aunt for a place to stay for the week, and I had no money. Really, I don't recommend this method of leaving home. I always was sort of pie-in-the-sky optimistic, though, so I knew it would work out, and it did.

Life is a highway. Right turns, wrong turns. All roads leading everywhere. I want to ride it, and I expect my son does, too.

33

Living Is Easy With Eyes Closed.... Strawberry Fields Forever

Every year, my husband and I set out to plant something new. Something in us drives us to spend entire weekends weeding, plotting, shoveling and planting in hopes that it will yield us something wonderful to set out on the dinner table.

And each year, without fail, we watch stuff wither and die or get eaten up by the local insect population. Our only success was the first year. We had such high ambitions for that 4 ft. x 8 ft. patch of raised garden. We planted a few tomato plants, four okra stalks, carrots, a watermelon, and a pineapple. My husband had some grandiose scheme by which we would grow another pineapple. Alas, this is not Hawaii and we are not pineapple growers.

Still, that little plot of garden yielded us fat, long okra pods all summer long, everyday. I fried up okra every week, and was still able to set some up for gumbo later that fall. We had plump, luscious tomatoes for months. That is, we had them after we finally taught Benjamin not to bring us the green ones. Well, even then, fried up, the green ones were delicious, too. "Fried green tomatoes" isn't just the name of a book and movie, folks.

The watermelon made it to the size of a cantaloupe, and when it looked as though the black ants were going to carry it away, we brought it inside and each had one slice. It was sweet and warm, and its seeds held all the promise of another watermelon in a few months.

But that was it. Every attempt thereafter has failed, though we've had great ambitions. Either we don't have the soil right, or we don't stop often enough in our busy day to give it more water... or any other host of reasons.

When did life become like that? When did I stop having enough time to do those things that are important to me? I haven't painted since Benjamin was a young child. I haven't taken photographs in forever. This summer, I'll do Thomas' senior portraits, but probably won't stop long enough to do landscapes or the scenes that bring so much happiness to me. I don't read regularly each evening, either. I suppose I can be grateful that at least I am writing.

This past weekend, Dennis and I put in a new, small garden. It's octagonal and we filled it with a rich dirt/compost mixture sure to grow all the strawberries we planted. I'm thinking about transplanting some Morning Glories that will twine up the bird feeder pole in the middle of the garden. Morning Glories, with their brilliant, large blue flowers will grow anywhere. I'll need something to look at when the strawberries die.

Ironically, my herbs, which I completely ignore, are still doing beautifully in January. Go figure.

34

Kiss My Tiara

For years, in spirit and in sass, some of my heroes have been a group of women who call themselves the Sweet Potato Queens. For me, they embody all that is truly feminine, southern, and spunky. Two years ago, I joined the ranks as a Sweet Potato Queen Wannabe-Wannabe and dolled myself up, drove to Jackson, and walked my sassy self in the big SPQ parade. Yes, I had the requisite big-haired red wig and ginormous black, sparkly sunglasses. My tiara, glittery lime green dress, and fishnets completed the costume. Never have I been so proud to put a crown on my head.

In the heart of nearly every southern girl is the desire to wear a crown at some important time in her life, whether literally or figuratively. For me, it was literally. That crown meant I was somebody to be fawned over. I felt immediately feminine and I felt powerful all at once. And those feelings didn't go away once I took the crown off.

I think sometimes people have a skewed vision of what it means to be feminine, especially when they view the south. They see helplessness and simple-mindedness. I see strength and tenacity. Do you have any idea how much self-control is involved in saying, "Well, bless your heart," as opposed to slapping someone hard across the face or cussing them out for their impertinence? Or how much patience is needed to create big hair and butterfly-wing eyelashes? And then there's all that sweet tea we have to make. Good Lord, a family of four can drink a dang gallon a day!

Then there's the SPQ motto: Be prepared and particular, on account of you just never know. That'll pretty much carry a woman through any circumstance.

Take my friend Judy, whose own motto is "Good girls go to heaven. Bad girls go everywhere."

Judy is marrying this stupendously nice-looking man in two weeks. This past weekend, I took her bridal portraits at a quaint little garden spot that's way out in the boonies. I must say, when I arrived to pick her up, she looked like a princess. Her tiara was already in place, and danged if she didn't look like she should wear a tiara everyday of her life.

After getting that glorious wedding dress on, Judy's precious little dachshund immediately walked up to the dress and proceeded to tinkle all over the beaded train. But did Judy scream and cry? No indeed. This is a woman who understands it's all about her, not the dress. We just sponged that dress off and it was right as rain in no time at all. Nor did she scream and cry when, right in the middle of taking pictures, she discovered a freshly dead opossum not two feet from her. In fact, all she said was, "My God, Evelyn, there's a fresh dead 'possum not two feet from me."

I say, who needs feminism? Now, I'm not talking about equality at the workplace, so don't get all bent out of shape with me. I believe I was given a brain, and by golly, I use it everyday.

Still, we treat our men good and in turn, they treat us like the queens God intended us to be. I don't even have to open my own door down at the Winn-Dixie - there's always a gentleman around to help a lady with that. And why in the world would I want to carry my own groceries just to prove how strong I am when that fine husband of mine, along with my teenage son, are more than willing? Furthermore, what's wrong with telling a man how much you admire those big muscles of his? Everybody likes to be treated special.

I suppose it boils down to this: a woman should be a woman enough to take care of herself and her own, and yet be feminine enough to allow herself to be treated like a queen.

I realize not every woman is going to agree with me, and to them, I'll just say, "Well, bless your sweet heart. You don't know what you're missing."

35

Though At Heart I'm a Pearl, I'm a Difficult Girl, So, Buddy, Beware

It's taken me many years to learn to laugh at myself. For all my earnestness about being a strong and independent southern woman, I will admit to my fair share of resulting embarrassments.

I pride myself on having designed and personally contracted the building of both houses we've owned. I know every corner, every piece of trim, every fixture, and in many cases, I worked on them myself. One of my dreams was to have a Jacuzzi bathtub so that I could relax at the end of a long workday.

Right after we moved in, I was ready for my first jet-infused bath. I love baths – bubbles, candles, soft music, good smelling oils, and a fluffy towel will usually bring me back to my sweet self in no time at all.

My husband wandered into the bathroom as the water for my bath was drawing. I was sitting in the tub and he uttered those ill-fated words: "Hon, do you know how to use the Jacuzzi?" My evil alter-ego raised its ugly head and snappily replied, "Do I look like an idiot? Do I look like someone who can't figure out how to use a simple bathtub!??" Dumb-stricken, my husband stood there as I turned on the jets.

Immediately, screaming ensued. Water was flying everywhere! The ceiling was soaking, the floor, the walls, the bathroom door, my hair, my husband - all were quickly getting wet. I desperately tried to cover the jets with my hands – never once considering that I should shut off the water – and ended up spraying my face and contact lenses. Off to the side, amidst my screams, I could hear my husband nearly choking he was laughing so hard, saying to himself all the while, "Do I LOOK like an idiot? Do I LOOK like an idiot? Hahahaha!!!" I finally found the off switch, and sat there with my hair dripping, mascara covering my face, leaving little black pools on my cheeks, as I looked around at the havoc I had just wreaked.

What my dear husband had been trying to tell me is that the water level has to be completely up over the jets before it can be turned on. The jets in front of me were covered, but the ones behind me were above the waterline. Just when I think I have it all together. :-)

36

My Son Turned Ten Just the Other Day

Much as I would like to stop time, it seems to move forward with a relentlessly ever-increasing speed. Already, it's Benjamin's birthday, and what a fine and good young man he has grown into. Yesterday, I held Benjamin as a small child; tomorrow, he'll be 10. Yesterday, I watched Thomas make elaborate forts with my sheets and furniture; today, he is officially a senior in high school. And both boys are so handsome. The other afternoon they were in the driveway washing the truck when two girls came by on bicycles. I was watering my flowers and watched the girls as they passed. One young lady almost fell off her bicycle as she rode by and kept an eye on them. I had to laugh.

Thomas took my car and drove it alone for the first time last night. Oddly enough, I was fine, but my husband looked at the clock again and again, all the while musing aloud, "Do you think we should call him?"

The first time my parents allowed me to take the car alone, I was sent on a short errand to the grocery store down the road. Halfway there, while driving on that two-lane country road, my tires went slightly off the asphalt and onto the soft shoulder, and I did what no driver should ever do - I over-compensated. Naturally, the car spun around and I ended up in the other lane going the wrong way. My parents STILL do not know about that.

Some days, especially lately, I long for that freedom to just get in the car and.... go. Drive. Take off. Follow a winding road. Be free from problems. Just when I thought everything would be all right with the thyroid diagnosis, the doctor came back and said I have diabetes now. Add anemia into the mix and there's little wonder about why I slept away three months of my life.

I'm looking forward to this summer. Already things have slowed down and my life outside has picked up. There are quiet evenings around the fire pit to continue enjoying; breakfast, dinner, and supper at the table on the porch to eat; afternoons in the pool to relax; birds and squirrels to watch; and children's laughter to listen to and their backyard games to watch. I can already tell everything's going to be all right.

37

For a Moment Like This, Some People Wait a Lifetime

"You're awfully jittery this morning," my husband fussed as we were driving around the French Quarter looking for a spot to park. "You don't understand; I've been waiting my whole life for this. I want it to go well," I replied, as calmly as I could.

I'd taken off this day from work months in advance in preparation for driving over to New Orleans with my oldest son so that we could take his senior pictures. The morning was hazy - not good picture weather -

but I knew that the haze would probably burn off by the time we arrived. Though still a bit foggy-looking, the day was beautiful.

Thomas' life revolves around the music he plays: the marching band, his own jazz band, the church band, and now in the recording studio he has built in our attic. As far as I could see, there was no other place in the world to have his pictures taken than in the Quarter - the heart of jazz.

We spent the better part of the morning getting some of the best shots ever near the levee and the riverboats, and we eventually wound our way around to Jackson Square. The square is filled to the brim with artisans, palm readers, mimes, and musicians, but the morning was still fresh and I suppose most musicians were still sleeping off the late night they'd had. There was one tuba player out there, though, and as we passed, he called out to Thomas, "Hey son, blow us a note!"

Thomas had been carrying his trumpet with him so that it could be in some of the photos we were taking. He looked over at me and I nodded my encouragement and then he walked over to the old man. "Can you lay down a B flat something or other - something or other like this for me: dum, dum, dum, dum, dum?" (That's my version of the music-speak going on.)

"How's this?" as the man began to play a low beat on the tuba. I guess it was fine because about five seconds later, my son began to play his shiny, silver trumpet. And what a song - he improvised for about five minutes, blowing the high notes, hitting the low long notes, screaming some of the other notes, and in general, putting on the performance of a lifetime.

Another old man, the tuba player's friend, stood up and got the gathering crowd to dance. Music began to fill every space in the air. People came out of shops, they came from restaurants, from the Cabildo, from the levee - they all ran to hear the wonderfully loud jazz concert going on. And all the while, his eyes closed, my son played on and on.

It occurred to me in those few minutes that never again would I be able to reproduce this very moment in time. This was a song that, because it was improvised, I would never hear again, this was a moment I would never experience again, and a time that would never, ever revisit me. And I reveled in it and drank it up, trying to absorb every second.

When the music was over, the large crowd laughed and cheered and put money into the Yellowtail Merlot wine box set out on the ground near the tuba player. So many people shouted out, hoping for more songs. But it was over. The moment had passed and we walked away, huge grins on our faces.

There are so many moments, so very many opportunities for things in my life to change at the drop of a hat. Embracing each new experience and saying goodbye to weights that linger in my life is a long and frequently painful process of growth. I say bring it on.

Thomas playing with Dr. Love in the Quarter.

About the Author

Evelyn Huckaby was born and raised in and around New Orleans, Louisiana. She currently resides in Baton Rouge, where she is a wife to Dennis and a proud mother to the two joys in her life, her sons, Thomas and Benjamin.

www.ingramcontent.com/pod-product-compliance
Lightning Source LLC
Chambersburg PA
CBHW051806040426
42446CB00007B/539